ABOUT THE A

David Mason, born 1960, studie
University before embarking on ... . training
with a pharmaceutical company. In 1992 he began work in
Alfresco Eating House. This decision to move to self
employment created the atmosphere for him to pursue his
interest in writing.

By the same author - 'Free Entertainment, a collection of poetic tales'.

First Published in 1996 in Great Britain by David J. Mason
Publishing Address:
Alfresco Eating House, Norwich Road, Ludham, Norfolk NR29 5QA.

British Library Cataloguing-in-Publication Data
A Catalogue record for this book is available
from the British Library.
© David J. Mason

ISBN 0 9521326 1 3

All rights reserved. No part of this book may be produced or utilised
in any form or by any means, electronic or mechanical, including
photocopying, recording, or by any information storage
and retrieval system without permission in writing
from the Publisher.

Produced in Great Britain by Skippers Print & Design
53a The Green, Martham, Great Yarmouth, Norfolk NR29 4PF.
Telephone: 01493 740998

Front Cover Illustration, 'Eye of the Storm' by Martin Walton.
Contact Address: Alfresco Eating House, Ludham, Norfolk

FOR THE INDIVIDUAL

CONTENTS:

PART ONE -
SOMETHING TO GET EXCITED ABOUT

Small Is Beautiful 8
Politics 9
Consumption 10
Not One Of Us 12
The Feel Good Factor 13
A Forgotten People 14
A Nation's Scrapbook 15
Just Do It! 16
To Recycle Or Not To Recycle 17
Death Of A Village 18
These Empty Streets 19
An Existence 20
Competition 21
It's Not For Me To Say 22
The Human Spectacle 23
90's Workplace 24
It's Not Working 25
Bored Room 26
Squeaky Clean 27
Signing Up 28
Don't Bank On It 30
Drug-U-Like 31

PART TWO - NATURE

The Waterfall 34
That Flowery Feeling 35
Hot Springs 36
Winter Life 37
Now You Feel It - Now You Don't 38
Buena Vista 39
The Nature Of Man's Rest 40
Burnt Out 41
Cold Cycle 42
The Untamed Sea 43

PART THREE - ALL IN THE MIND

In The Mood 46
Life's Quest 47
Someone Else 48
Fear 49
The Here And Now 50
Restless 51
All At Sea 52
Undermined 53
Strive 54
Beyond 55
The Workings Of The Mind 56
A Rest 57

PART FOUR - LOVE

Two Onto One 60
The Love Token 61
Love Is A Drug 62
Coffee 63
Lips 64
Love In A Kiosk 65
Let Me Cry 66
The Words I Say 67
Lying In Wait 68
Turn The Light Off Darling 69
Your Scent 70
The Buxom Blond 71

PART FIVE - PEOPLE AND PLACES

Ride On, Ride On 74
Street Cafe 76
Magaluf 77
Eric 78
The Texan 79
The Unwelcome Guest 80
Johnny Wharton 82
Stan 83

PART SIX - POEMS NOT INCLUDED IN PARTS 1,2,3,4 AND 5

An End To Anorexia 86
The Gut 87
The Spillage 88
Dumped 90
Shopping For Shoes 91
The Race 92
Tightrope 94
Chewing Gum, Brace And Teeth 95

28/6/96

Best Wishes,
Dave

PART ONE

SOMETHING TO GET EXCITED ABOUT

SMALL IS BEAUTIFUL

To have more of what we want,
Not what we need.
Westernism, consumerism,
Anything but greed.

A drug prescribed by the media,
An ideal at any age.
Capture the thoughts of an innocent man
And put him in a cage.

"Successes" are born every minute,
Aspiring to have and to hold.
Their mothers and fathers look up to them,
Few of them bought and not sold.

"Failures" find it hard to ignore
The judgement prevailing these days.
A remnant believe in themselves repeating
"There's more, more, more than one way."

A hard fact, money is time,
Snared in death by our term.
We may at least loose the cuffs
By buying the freedom we earn.

It takes radical thinking,
A now and not then.
Share more and spend less,
Goodwill to all men.

POLITICS

Talk, talk, talk - we all fall down,
Our ignorance - your intellect.
We cannot comprehend
The depth of your answers.

From studio and radio car,
Your salve to calm a troubled nation.
You wash your hands of us,
We bathe in your hypocrisy.

Faultless, measured you deliver
Words we don't collect and store.
Our hopes live on as we forget
The promise of great things to pass.

When you have finished with your world
I turn again to mine.
Come, deliver me from all evil,
Tune in again same place, same time.

CONSUMPTION

Magnified Bacilli* swim
In their tubercular sea,
Rotting rods creating chaos,
Pus-filled, putrid alveoli.

This slice of death,
Behold we see
The nature of mortality.

In formalin pickle split asunder,
A coroner's case will never rest.
Doctors wash hands, dispose of the doubt,
The secrets of science exposed in this chest.

Fresh air, a change of circumstance,
A chance to breath new life
Under clear blue skies of some Alpine land,
Away from the thrust of a surgeon's knife.

Up there the air too thin for him,
His heaving lungs sucked in the gas.
Then the setting sun on the pallid corpse,
The hour of truth had come to pass.

*Bacillli - Bacteria or 'Rods' present in lung cells infected by tuberculosis

Televised, the foreign bodies
In their familiar famine.
Disease amongst the living dead,
It pays not to examine.

This hopeless hell,
Behold we see
The sin of mans avidity.

Thumbing through your blank accounts
It seems you have still more to pay.
It's in your interest we extort
The money you can't raise today.

We'll give you hope and sell you aid,
Would you like to buy our tanks?
Whilst people starve you feed their food
Through the gaping jaws of the world's great banks.

Our economic growth has slowed,
You must learn to fight it out.
We'll save ourselves and watch you bleed
-Consumption kills without a doubt.

NOT ONE OF US

I've seen the fella shaking slippery hands
With those who'd constitute his fans.
He's made to appeal to the middle classes,
Whilst his heart pumps the blue of a bloody fascist.

The saviour of upstanding society he,
Beware those scrounging security.
Blame the husbandless mother, the black and the poor
-Without this type around you would have so much more.

People believed his simplistic view
And voted for him and his rhetoric too,
But this is the man whom we failed to see
Has no time for things of the ordinary.

He's too busy building a power base,
Ignoring the street man who gave him his place
And what is this leaking - consultancy?
Working six jobs or more - hypocrisy!

He's still trying to kid us, he's upright and strong,
That he has it right and we've got it all wrong,
But I never expected humility
From this God far removed who fails to see ....

THE FEEL GOOD FACTOR

I have to tell the unmentioned sin,
The feel good factor is missing within.
But what makes it worse, you will not want to know,
If you gave me more money it still would not show.

Though human nature, there reaches a limit
To caring for self and excluding the spirit.
Deny a response to my struggling brothers,
Believe I'm elitist, to hell with the others.

I'm tired of being told what to do,
As a nation we need to be ruling, not ruled.
We need to discuss us, you must hear our voice,
Your circus democracy give us no choice.

I won't feel better till dawneth the day
You listen to what the majority say.
Don't let your politics get in the way,
You must look to the future, not always today.

A FORGOTTEN PEOPLE

Seven out of ten
Won't work again,
We've fenced them in
Their slum of a pen.

Where dreams are of hope,
Of enough just to cope,
But this hope is a joke,
Slithering down the familiar slope.

No mobility, no phone,
In hell all alone.
No wonder drugs are done,
Bringing life to the bone.

Alarm bells ringing,
Sirens singing,
We are bringing
The message of the dead to the living.

A NATION'S SCRAPBOOK

Your likeness appears in early text
And many similar
Fill the following pages,
Glued firmly in their place.
No solvent, all is bankruptcy,
Stuck against a backdrop
Of an eerie gloom.
A wasteland
Of hopeless pessimism,
Fear of living
Trapped in tangled wire,
More are added to the volume.
Day by day disparity
Invades each higher order,
The net cast further
Up the echelons of society.
But gentlemen are not at risk,
No need to read between the lines,
To them life is a closed book.

JUST DO IT!

In Brazil there was a summit
Where they'd blow the eco trumpet
And find out just who dunnit,
Let the ozone levels plummet.

They made all sorts of pleas,
Like save the hardwood trees,
Harbour natural energies
And stop dumping in the seas.

World population growth must slow.
Poverty and wars must go.
In poor countries crops will grow
As we share around the seed to sow.

We'll set targets for emission rate,
Reach them by a certain date.
Won't leave mankind to its' own fate,
Take action less we are too late.

TO RECYCLE OR NOT TO RECYCLE

The sheer excitement of what you might find,
The secrets of the skip
Filled with offerings from a throw-away nation.
Rubbing shoulders with a wealth of rubbish,
Furniture forlorn,
Fickle owners following new fashions,
Consumer goods consumed,
Waiting in working order.
There it remains, the presiding view,
Disinterred might decrease demand.
Economists tell us that won't do,
The world's free markets have it all planned.

DEATH OF A VILLAGE

Bystanders witness the agonising demise
Of a pre-war corner store that was Clarks and then Smiths
But now lies
White wash windowed in pathetic guise.
Where once was provided all that was needed,
No more bargain buys.
Once vital minutes spent forging our ties
-A lifeline, the hub of our daily routine,
A community dies.

We are channelled to our friendly hyperstore
Placed upon a tranquil rural greenfield site,
But no more.
From closet boardroom they came and saw
And conquered by crossing palms of upright men
Who knew the score.
With buying power they wage their war,
Shopping made sterile, efficient and easy
As never before.

We're shopping in droves, we're the modern kind,
Enticed by the loyalty cards
We find
Ourselves driven by a change of tide
Which washes away all our yesterday
-A movement of time.
And as I reflect on this new design
I wonder aloud, was I given the chance
To make up my mind.

THESE EMPTY STREETS

Down these empty streets,
The gloom has sat upon
Empty footpaths.
The cold still pressed against
Tight shutters.
A desolate fog filled
Each tiny space.

Where are the living?
Clamped inside these warm shells?
Safe from the frosty fall out,
Averse to the icy sensation.
Numbed by nature,
Bred in these cages.
Suburbia is sleeping,
Awaiting Monday's shot gun start.

Down these empty streets
I wander
And wonder
At the lively ticking of my mind.

AN EXISTENCE

A dry land
Where burning ambition
Drank deep
Of river bed,
Springs silenced
Where passion flowed
Once cropping ideas
On fertile fields,
Now crusted and barren,
Blistered in this bright new age.
Encroaching desert
Preys upon fallow land.
The picture has never been clearer.
-Not a cloud on the horizon,
No-one weeps
Over a lost cause.
Yet out at sea
A storm may gather,
The boat rocked,
It sweeps inland.
Rumblings of discontent
Stir the dull and lifeless,
Anarchy reigns.
Shoots of seeds long planted
Spring forth with joy.

COMPETITION

We're all the same, the rich, the poor,
But frail perception undermines,
What you wear and what you're worth
Has dulled our leaden minds.

I look upon the shining stars,
At those who would eclipse my sun,
Straining hard to see the light,
Save my sinking as a stone.

Working late I'm down not out,
Riches earned and a penny saved.
A designer life to live and feed,
A conditioned fear I must evade.

And what of you my running mate?
You are my saving grace.
In your pathetic lowly state,
I can look you in the face.

IT'S NOT FOR ME TO SAY

Strange the suddenness of events
Overtaking my Saturday afternoon stroll.
Through southern suburbia,
Patrolling familiar pavements,
Echoing in empty air
To a stampede of boots
Skidding to a halt.
Yelling, a mound of flailing flesh,
Then a towering circle
Above the crumpled heap.
The alien cries,
The feet fly at him.
He is black and blood
Is flowing
And he yells at me
And the white faces turn
Towards their judge.
I can understand their view,
Always two sides to a story.
They don't have to ask,
I move off, into the shadows of this sunny afternoon.

THE HUMAN SPECTACLE

The tunnel vision boring deep
Into your head
Causes you a sideways glance,
Then a deep, deep stare,
Meditating upon the gravity that is me.
Unlike all else that has gone before you
I have disturbed
Your train of thought,
Stationary at the buffers.
But not mine,
For shocking though I appear,
So abnormal you cannot bear to pass me by,
I am thinking,
Foaming at my mouth.
The words won't come,
But in the flying spittle
I am condemning your world.

90'S WORKPLACE

A war has been declared.
Ordinariness the fashion today,
Charisma, a little too risqué.
Yes I know it was once admired
But then we would only tolerate
Charisma, strictly second rate.
And now we've nearly wiped it out,
We've cut out all the fun,
This is the age of industrial robot, politics has won.
No escaping the mould,
Those that do are told
Their helping hand is no longer required
Or their chance of promotion has just expired.
Objectivity, the disease endemic,
Performance related, work that is worth it.
Only the ruthless and cunning survive,
While the guys with charisma quit or retire.

IT'S NOT WORKING

Middle managers meddling,
Order tedious tasks.
Political players producing paper,
Shifting statistics - sod all use.
Respected, revered, right on.
Valued veneer of reputable raiment.
Ambitious, amoral, avoiding.
Treacle trails slip away.

Money maketh our modern man,
Warping values of western works.
Ideals sit uneasy with the earthbound,
'Til soaring we shall see God's gifts.

BORED ROOM

You can't
Speak to someone in a meeting.
You can only
Try again later.
You might
Want to leave a contact number.
They won't
Return your call.
You wish
They'd stop messing you about.
You can guess
What it's all about.

From the shelter of your frozen phone box,
You imagine
Their ermming and arrahing.
You understand
The unimportance of their gathering.

You've been there
Drawing patterns on headed notepaper.
Time taught you
To keep a clean sheet.

But when they break,
It's a different story.
Something must be done
-The lunch time sandwich decided upon.

SQUEAKY CLEAN (An evening at McDonalds)

I saw her spraying immaculate table tops,
Wishing away the make-believe mess
On the surface,
Spotless before her scrubbing started.

And the trays
In their slots,
And the bins
Of black bags.
All were washed clean
And hidden from view.

Tirelessly she keeps order
Where motes of dust might fly,
Sterilising seats on which
Her customers sat,
Wiping away their finger marks,
Moving to the tune of Lloyd-Webber,
Whose veneer of sound
Applies the final polish.

SIGNING UP

Where's the fire in the belly?
The stiff upper lip?
Trembling at this expert
Shooting from the hip.
Into the soft spirit,
Your Achilles heel,
The private sanctum,
Fear made real.

What have you put by?
What securities have you?
The words of our expert,
A worldly view.
Exposes your lack,
Darkens your mind,
Cloning forth worries
Of a monetary kind.

And what about death?
Your dependants at sea?
The Thespian expert
Feels sadness for me.

And what of your youth?
I'm afraid it won't last,
Our philosopher expert
Says age catches fast.

I forgot the old maxim
"Live life for today",
I trust and believe
What the experts say.

All was clear then,
There was no better time.
The experts have helped me,
My life's on their line.

DON'T BANK ON IT

I know not whence these figures came,
The minus signs which lay the blame
On me, who has fed fat the same,
Wasted in the shadow of the bank's weight gain.

I thought I had worked hard enough
And now they send me all this stuff.
Your friendly lender must get tough.
We want it back, life can be rough.

How come your pockets bulge with cash?
A question I should dare to ask,
Then scold myself for being rash.
The banks have always had the stash.

I accept my sentence and so fear
The passing of successive years,
The slipping chain of my life's gears,
The hope you promised disappears.

I've heard you help the richer few,
Bringing them more riches too.
It's simple all they have to do -
Invest and prosper - save with you.

But all the goods you laid aside
-Your house, your car, your joy and pride,
They've disappeared - the bank has died,
The system took you for a ride.

I dreamt I had great wealth instead,
The manager said "Use your head"
But I'm tired of feeding, I want to be fed
-Make sure my stash stays under the bed.

DRUG-U-LIKE

To sniff or scratch or swallow or snort,
To convey the weapon
Seeping through membrane, pushing through stream
Of blood tainted.
Arriving at organs molested by molecules
The body sees fit
To chuck out, adding turmoil
To a system stressed
By the everyday whirl of living.
This hell in my head,
It should be outlawed.
Those cells pushing messenger hormones,
Proteins upsetting my body's balance,
Leaving me powerless,
Moody at their mercy.
Why should I refrain
From counter attack?
This is chemical warfare,
I must decide my strategy
To destroy the enemy within.

PART TWO
NATURE

THE WATERFALL

A weakness developed,
It was the earth's fault.
Rocks rubbing together
Collapse and a funnel forms
Where finger leafed ferns
Fill clefts of rock,
Rising perpendicular from pool side.
From their galleries they see
Underground waters surface as streams
Sliding along hanging stems stretching,
Stretching
Into the abyss,
This foaming pot spewing forth,
Sick with the constant feeding
From tireless cascade
Pouring over the pouting lip.

THAT FLOWERY FEELING

Convulvulus, beguiling colours.
Wraps itself around,
By nature strangles,
Can stop the breathing
Or clasp aorta,
A surgeon's clamp.

First flower then fruit,
Green bananas taste bad
But worse
Can fracture skulls.
One may not be conscious
Of these missiles hidden on high.

There are colours made to shock
The system, seeing new species
Of rich colour and rare combination.
Wild eyes dilating,
Messages throb through nervous lines,
Electrical overload, system breakdown.

Look but do not touch
Poisoned fruits bright with dark centres
Of sickly castor oil
Or maturing bean
Of bitter coffee,
But today life is sweet.

HOT SPRINGS

Furtively we undress in the dark,
Peeling away the daytime shroud,
Making ready for the ceremony,
Contemplating a miracle
Beyond the depth
Of these holy waters.

A silent scream of delight,
Alien warmth befriending the body.
A steaming soak
Stripping worn flesh
To flow over bone,
Making a soft sponge.
Easing between cartilage,
Eeking out pain
With an oily balm,
Numbing those gnawing nerves.

Unlocking the tight tiredness of muscle,
Freeing fibres knotted,
Stressed by skeletal order.
So then the final parting,
As an airship setting sail,
Completing the experience,
Mind separated from body.

WINTER LIFE

Feet splaying on the sucking mud.
Constantly shifting power of balance
Until I reach the earth's crust,
Terra firma of permafrost.
This warm tunnel
Hemmed about by hedge.
Home to a hypothermic squirrel,
Frozen in a tree crook,
Gob stopped with acorn
And to a massive rat
Scurrying a hundred yard dash,
Winking undercover.

Across a field of folded earth,
Chilling air fights down the throat.
Swallowing missile snowflakes,
Bowed over avoiding a head on.
Out on the marsh, sedge and grass,
Sentries with waving flower heads,
Guard dykes from hissing wind.
And behind a tar baby tree
Holds forth black fingers
Like some carboniferous relic.
Atop a crow caws
Making a blue tear in this sullen sky.
No reprieve, patched up
He later pours forth scorn,
Once more the white settles.

NOW YOU FEEL IT - NOW YOU DON'T

Heavy boots mince powder ice,
An incessant crunching,
Rhythm of an Arctic explorer.
Primeval pacing sends pulses
Connecting body, then mind
To earth's core below.
Beyond the sound of marching
Eyes are scanning a novel vision.
Thistle heads are land-locked urchins,
Reeds mope beneath their heavy winter shell.
Every shoot has its' crystalline case,
White needles pierce the air.
There is no yielding,
The sun seems powerless to melt
This frozen armour,
Thickening in the twilight of the day.

This is a moving picture.
An armada of fleeing ducks
Skids amongst the shadows,
Fading from the banks of the river.

Yet it is essentially still.
Photographers clear away tripods of testimony.
A mantle of mist settles
And like the redundant windmills,
The mind is frozen.
As the ice beneath gives way to earth,
The footfall is cushioned,
There is no way of measuring time and motion.

BUENA VISTA

Climbing, I follow a path to the cross,
At its' platform end transfixed I stare.
Manufactured in metal, the Saviour's loss,
His insignia left but he is elsewhere.

I was not alone, there was someone there with me,
Perhaps The Way, The Truth, The Light,
His breath then whispered "I'll help you to see"
I will turn you to the right.

I tiptoed to the rock's edge,
Curtain branches pulled aside
And I teetered on the high ledge
-My vista deep and wide.

A perfect bowl for Mother Earth,
Restful greens bewitched the eye.
The basin was lined with a spongy turf,
The fingers of trees stretched up high.

I wanted to dwell in this perfect land
But descent is Hell at best.
I hung on my shelf, turned my back on the plan,
Kept the secret inside my chest.

THE NATURE OF MAN'S REST

I heard my Mother calling,
Could not look back
To those spring torrents making deep
The pools of blue.
Heaving hillsides sighed,
Valleys empty, echoed the reply,
Our Son, our Son, is gone away,
He is lost to another land.

The heat held tight within her bosom,
Her branches hung
With the garlands of summer.
She commands
All that can fly to fly
And the crawling cacophony
Rustles out a welcome,
Vibrance in the dappled light,
Smoothing stone and moss.

I have made for you
This path of life.
Your footfall fills
These friendly corridors.
All this room is yours.
I have made your bed
And you shall lie in it,
Soothed by the balm of my sunset.

Now we have made our peace
When again shall you return?
I dare to want to stay with you
"How long?" I ask, the next sojourn.

BURNT OUT

The striking sun is
Melting tarmac
And his prints are upon
The parched fields,
Reflecting the yellow face,
Unwelcome in these parts.

Air thick with heat,
A listless layer
Sitting heavy to stifle
A murmur from the land,
Where once sea breezes
Cut through the balmy seal.

The jelly muscles
Turning mole hills to mountains.
Relentless request
To grind upon the pedals.
An errant cyclist dreams
Of water and of rest.

COLD CYCLE

For fully five minutes
A warm core
Stands alone
Against the enveloping cold.
Peeling away frozen layers,
Life sweeping through limbs
So that the heart pumps gladly,
Pushing power through pedal and crank,
Turning tyres on gritty diamond rime,
A fizzing of wheel on black ice.
The smallest descent
Sends mist marauding,
Cold vice clamping,
Dank and almost dark.
Above it all
A pale red sun
Sentenced to hanging,
Dying, slowly down.

Dazzling headlights illuminating ruddy visage
Channelled with streams of sweat.
When the pounding stops
The blood may thicken and turn to ice,
So take this frozen cyclist
And store at room temperature.

THE UNTAMED SEA

One day the mill pond carried no curse,
Its' translucent waters beckoning a steady stroke
Along the causeway central to the frame
-Surround of rising rock giving way to mountain tops.

Another day there is a roaring from far off.
A terrible rumble of undercurrent
Flagrantly beating weathered walls of a cage,
A sea held prisoner at bay.

Yesterday he held you aloft in his salty arms.
Today he would hurl you skyward, grind your bones.
In his raging he has murdered men
But he will not be locked away.

What saviour will assuage his anger?
Stop this kicking sand and spitting seaweed?
I want to swim with him again,
Oh God, save his tortured soul!

PART THREE
ALL IN THE MIND

IN THE MOOD

What is sad?
What is happy?
It makes me sad
To think I won't be happy again.
I'm so happy,
I dread the thought of sadness.
Good things make me happy,
Bad things make me sad.
But is there anything good
About being happy?
Is there anything bad
About being sad?
It makes me happy to know I feel,
I should be sad if I didn't.

LIFE'S QUEST

In the womb,
No insider information
On life's dealing.
My first breath,
They respond
In another language.
When I learn to speak
I realise
They have no answers.
Then I learn to think
But age
Overtakes my mind.
Still I travel in
The right direction,
Which is backwards,
And am relieved to know
Death's utterance,
"Life's sentence never made sense."

SOMEONE ELSE

Had enough?
Tired of torment?
No torch in the tunnel?
Contemplating self destruction?

Answer ad
Fill in facts
For photofit
Personality profile.

Returning reply
Found a fellow
You can fit in
All fixed
Transfer deadline
Last chance
No life to lose
Another's to gain.

I've done it
I'm him
I peer out
From his shell.

But inside a shadow
Of my former self
Clouds every mood
I make.

FEAR

You cry at birth,
I will haunt you for the rest of your days.
I do so with all my subjects,
You must learn to master me.
A sense of perspective is what you require,
What is the worst fate I harbour?

You must decide between adventure and I.
Choose the former, I am hidden backstage,
Allow me to star and I will run the show,
Adrenalin assisted, the heart hiccuping,
The heat of sweat, the sinking soul.
I will torture as long as you allow.

Dismiss me, scoff in my face,
For the most part I am a shadow.
Cloud your thoughts and I will grow in you,
Rain will fall and ruin you.
Keep your eyes toward the light,
Fixed on the sun, where I cannot abide.

THE HERE AND NOW

You cannot live in the yesteryear.
You are tempted
To imagine you can.
But wait - those moments
You can recall
Place, time, people, scene,
But mood is missing.
Exposed, as in a vacuum
Empty of atmosphere.
Hopelessly beyond.
The one-off experience
Feeling far removed
Forever.

A collection of faded images.
What use?
Nourishing the whole
And, on occasion revealed
To the delight of others.
Finally a template
For future design.

RESTLESS

I've needed some time
To step out of line,
Search depths of my mind
To face what I'd find,
But on and on the pantomime,
Too late, I had ignored the signs.
Too busy, too full,
Too narrow and dull,
Of work and of care
And nothing to spare,
Life's leisure was rare
Because I did not dare.
I've stacked up my wealth,
They say I've good health
But I've lost the key
To set my life free
-I cannot be
Just me, you see.

ALL AT SEA

Drowning in deep waters,
Mine and mine alone,
Icy to the touch,
Chilling on the bone.
A dark descent of jet black,
An oily whirlpool
Sucking at the innocent
So afraid to sink
Without a trace.

Wave ahoy there!
Lifeguards on parade,
Strong and supple,
Quick to save.
Young and handsome,
Bright and brave.
Flying like fish,
Leaping the swell.
Here I am!
They flag and flounder.
I curse and
Hear their cries,
"We tried to save you
But we cannot save ourselves"

All at sea
And not a lifebelt between us.

UNDERMINED

It took years
To dig this tunnel,
So many thoughts
To make secure.
The painstaking planning,
The careful procedures
Learnt from lessons of grief,
From tortuous experience.
I have fashioned a save haven,
A padded cell
Full of supplies
Of every kind
You could possibly need.

One day disaster strikes.
The smell of stagnant air,
Of my own sweat,
Of still wet warmth.
I look around
Surveying my burrow,
My quiet life
Collapsed before me
As it has
Many times before
And will
Many times again.
In the mean time
I must take up my shovel
And dig.

STRIVE

Something other than what I am
I'm afraid I can't deliver,
Just this sordid self
For you to contend with
Like myself, every passing day
Relentless replays of my record.
So here I am
No flip side,
Nothing new but
Crackling and grating
And the words hard to find
Above the background noise.
So everything turns a little bland
And neither of us are amused
But crave a change
Which, even if it comes,
Will leave you wanting more.

BEYOND

Beyond the dawn,
Beyond the sunset,
Above the clouds,
Below the earth.
Hidden chambers of self,
Fleeting images float therein,
Show themselves at night
While the rest is sleeping.
And in this subconscious cave
We explore the extraordinary,
The treasured gold as of a ring
Which we may wear or cast away.
Without it the mirror deforms,
Blunts our cutting edge
And the spirit dies,
For the spirit is beyond reason.

THE WORKINGS OF THE MIND

Picture a pool,
Crystal clear waters
Over lacy fronds of wavy green,
Like the wiring in the mind.
And the calm fluid
Of the brain's ventricles,
Easing the stimulus.
Lapping, a gentle tide,
Brings forth a host of creation.
Ideas spawn and swim in the light.
A storm!
The waters turn turbid,
Power lines are down,
The machine barely functioning.
Wait for its passing,
For repair and renewal.
Do not reflect on these troubled waters,
For in them you will never see yourself.

A REST

Looking out over the sun
I would rise above it, weightless,
Dropping anchor on this turning globe.
Motionless at high noon,
I would accommodate nothing,
Lose all sense
Of being, beat and pulse,
Of blood and flesh.
I am a museum piece
Stricken by siesta,
Tired of turning out
Day after day.
Turning into an angel
Or a ghost,
I'll let you know
When I begin again.

PART FOUR
LOVE

TWO ONTO ONE

Noah started the rot.
Male and female,
They came in two by two,
Not one, was allowed on board.
We have singularly failed
To promote oneness,
Doubling back,
Pre-pairing ourselves for life.
Two join as one,
But then one splits in half.
One part dies,
Semi-detached.
The fraction left to fend
In a world twice its' size.
Some choose solitude,
Others fail to find a match.
Do your bit for the individual,
For surely
One day
You will find yourself numbered amongst them.

THE LOVE TOKEN

Woken
By the shattering
Of cut glass
On polished stone
To find the red rose she gave
Gulping air,
Shuddering cold,
Drying to death, dismembered,
A loss of petal limbs.
Traces of carnage litter tiles.
Contemplating my loss,
The cat creeps in placing
A friendly paw upon me, whispers
"It would never have lasted anyway".

LOVE IS A DRUG

The beautiful body calls to me,
Wooing me away from the worries of work,
The stresses and strains of loveless interludes,
To the willing warmth,
The womb of your bed,
Where entwined with you I renew
My strength from the energy of your embrace.
Coiled in a nest of naked limbs,
Bathing in a stream of kisses,
Pecking like love's acupuncture.
Locked together we live
In a soft world
Of waving summer wheatfields,
Of endless sunshine and eternal life.
Leaving you I gaze upon your beauty,
Fighting to remember our's is the real world.

COFFEE

You invited me in
To taste your boiling brew
And gave me something more,
We both expected you to.
And I don't care for caffeine,
Not in the afternoon
Or evenings when I shake
But I swoon
At the thought of steam
Rising in the bedroom,
Your hot milky lips
Igniting passion's bomb.
So tell me again
What I came for,
"Just a quick coffee
Nothing more."

LIPS

Across the divide,
The humming hot air,
You are mincing idle words
For a far away friend.
Why deceive yourself?
Your's would be the pleasure
If you told the whole world
You loved me,
And you do.
For in the blink of an eye
You shed such light
Upon your subject,
Who will surely reciprocate
At a second glance,
Following the passion
Of your first.

Oh the undercurrent!
The heat of this moment
Wired for romance.
To this day
You never swore it
But I know that you love me,
I saw the lips move.

LOVE IN A KIOSK

Opens up the red box,
Easing herself against smooth glass,
Hand curled about the mouthpiece,
Sighs,
To calm.
Expressive of innocence
Her face won't move a muscle
Until his response
And then
An explosion of smile,
Of white teeth
And wet lip.

Speech slows,
He woos her.
As the chatter stops
Fingers feel through hair,
Hands on hips and thighs
As she coils
For more comfort,
At once a sensual snare.

She has him,
Her face says so.
And back on the street
Her body sways with success.

LET ME CRY

The tears of a man will not out,
The pain not apparent
Until X-rays show a broken heart,
Shattered by a shot of love.
Drilled to soldier on
In an emotional war
Which took me prisoner,
Sworn to secrecy.
The tears are salty concentrate
That wells and flows
Behind closed doors,
Where love and life run red.
I sink to my depths,
Drawing forth this deadly reserve
And in lancing this poison
I take comfort
In the boy I have become.

THE WORDS I SAY

Words I surely meant to say,
Bold as brass on printed page,
Jumping into the afflicted eye,
Stricken by passing winters.
Cataract covers give a dim view,
Taking the edge away.
I loved you and my life began
But ended soon afterwards
When we could not live the promises
Or speak these written words,
The dry dust in our throats
Bereft of fertile feeling.
I love you but the song is not the same.
I'm singing out of tune,
Marching out of time,
Living a different life,
Waiting for a break
Between this story and the next.

LYING IN WAIT

She felt
Out of sorts
And rolled
On her side,
Her sighs
Tell it all.
She dreams.
I take flight
And wait
For bright sunlight.
Her mind
A grey cloud,
Deep despair.
Her living alone
With me
On the edge
Of leaving
Before we both
Bleed to death.

TURN THE LIGHT OFF DARLING

With the light on
I think I see your real self.
In the shadows
I doubt your existence.
In the dark
I grope about searching
For your form, checking,
Reassuring myself in shapes
And in the quivering of your body
I am left guessing at the gulf between us.
You retreat to the cover of sheets,
The black of your burrow,
And moving on you
I am left grasping
At the illusion of lovemaking.

YOUR SCENT

Mauling this mound of wool and cotton,
Searching for some new suit to put on,
I stop to admire the mine you once wore
Which belongs to you, soaked with your perfume.
I bury my face in your breast,
Your arms tie tight around me.
You smother me with you,
My heart leaps to your essence.
I wear your heart on my sleeve,
Cloth myself in your majesty,
Dream again of touching
The skin inside this shell,
Of turning scent into sense,
Smell into touch
-And cheat on you,
Peeling you away
To expose myself
Naked to another's caress.

THE BUXOM BLOND

Shows a deep cleavage
Polished with passion,
The curves clinging,
Contained in their treasure chest.
The key to success
Could declare the contents
Of luscious flesh
In milky white.
She carries her load aloft
And her bosom pals
Feel themselves falling
Headfirst into
Her pillowy secrets.

PART FIVE
PEOPLE AND PLACES

RIDE ON, RIDE ON

Jesus proclaims "Cuenta conmigo",
Protective arms beseeching our trust.
And as the bus lurches to start
I am trusting in this icon,
This sticker with a beatific smile
Smoothing the driver's hard nosed stare.

Driven at breakneck speed,
Puppet heads are jerked tight
On invisible strings,
As sleeping passengers are blind
To the pitfalls, many potholes
Make bus swerve.

And then the breakdown.
A hoard of surgeons,
Spanner and screwdriver
Wrenching at the black bolts.
The patient breathes again,
Smoke and cinders fly.

The terrain changes.
Like a sleek fish
The bus swims downstream,
Jumping narrow bridges,
Gaining momentum
For the upstream struggle.
Tyres feeling for the tarmac edge
Ending with a sheer drop below.

Journey's end, cross the valley floor.
A smooth finish brings a sigh of relief.
People planning the rest of their lives
Step once more on solid ground.
The majestic beast has delivered,
Just as Jesus promised.

STREET CAFE (San Jose)

The toucan vendor blows hard,
Streams of whistles from the wooden bird.
Street sellers wait for the roving eye,
They fix it, you focus upon their display.
Politely you hear them, your mind cast astray,
Then shaking a head you are turning away
To be met by another enquiry,
A shoe shine for you or your lady?
Here it is where the Ticos roam,
Las turistas content in their transient home.
This is a set up for observation,
The cast comprising every nation.
Some drink, some smoke, some write, all stare
At this microcosm of global fayre.

MAGALUF

Every day's a winner
Down in Magaluf.

In Lineker's and Benny Hill's
We're drinking bargain beer
And spewing all the night away
Leaving trails there and here.

There's Cornish pasty chips and beans
And tea just like your Mum makes.
There's none of that there foreign stuff,
Just buttered scones and fancy cakes.

There's sun and sand and sex galore,
Sombreros, donkeys, leather
And we like it 'cos it's England
Except for better weather.

Every day's a winner
Down in Magaluf.
I know 'cos I've stayed there,
I am the living proof.

ERIC

It's 7am I hear the banging,
The rice pan gong of deadened tone.
He means no harm, he's just hanging
About in the back yard.

A solemn posture calls to prayer,
His body contorts, bent over the mat.
There's nothing wrong in his kneeling there
Pious at the back door.

We are juxtaposed on the village street,
After twelve months silence he speaks.
Then mornings after I'd watch to greet
Him waving in the back yard.

There were mood swings, voices circumspect,
The night with the woodcutter's axe.
He showed me the motorcycle wrecked,
Broken in the back yard.

But the tide of change was flowing fast,
There was breaking and entering and clearing his place.
They threw out the history, buried the past
In the back yard.

This holy of holies was no longer censored,
The first time he invited me into his house.
He smiled and shook my hand as I entered
Through the front door.

THE TEXAN

Push aside the unmarked door,
Gaze habitually toward tiled wall.
Concentrate on the job in hand,
A reduction in volume, no matter how small.

In the gully below a cockroach climbs
Escaping the acid rain.
One false move from either of us
And his life is down the drain.

Then a big guy bursts in
Heavy breathing and hissing.
Our cockroach stops sharp
To avoid being pissed on.

Spit away the cigar butt,
Enquire as to where I came from.
"Old England", I jest and I look for a smile
But the joke's not that funny - and there's none.

"Texas" came the gruff reply,
Well I thought I had better ask.
There followed an awkward silence,
Zipping up I should finish my task.

"You like Costa Rica, you like it here?"
He grimaced and spat in the sink.
"It's dirty, it's backward I'm leaving here."
Say it's great to know what you think!

THE UNWELCOME GUEST

Like Russian roulette,
One invitation loaded
But we must party
At any cost.
You have your suspicions
And I mine.
I say it's never the quiet one
But the loud laughing sort,
Embryonic party animal
Growing in size and volume,
Trading spirit for spirit,
All your booze.
The party parasite
Offers up his four ring pulls
On the alter of grace,
Receiving freely from kitchen table.

He's such a scream
On circus parade.
The faux pas embodied,
Excused through the excesses.
Tiring of this sport,
Others allow him to fade away.
No more nurturing,
Left to fend for himself.
Retreats to the corner
Passing in and out
Of the atmosphere.

Through a haze
The sinking eyes,
The slurring mouth denying.
"I'll be alright"
"I'm OK"
Then the body judders,
The volcano active,
Yellow-orange lava
On couch and carpet.

The evidence removed,
Upstairs we place the package.
It must have moved
At sometime,
For in the early hours
It is found in your bed
And will remain there
For some time to come.

JOHNNY WHARTON

Picked snot
And showed you the lot
In a green and black hand
And just as he planned
You're shocked you yuk
But you can't resist another look.
Johnny belched good
And after milk the letters would
Echo forth from his tunnel throat
And to see our disgust made Johnny gloat.
And to promise a show much more perverse
He would start at the "Z" and burp in reverse.
He spat
You knew that
But you really didn't mind
'Cos Johnny was harmless and one of a kind.
And you knew in the future all that he'd done
Could be recalled in poems just like this one.

STAN

Stan the man
Close up a fright,
He just might
Swallow you whole.
Not his intention,
It's fair to mention.
Can't keep away,
His face in your face.
A puppet head performing
Can be quite alarming.
Stan is joie de vivre,
Emanating energy
At something over eighty,
The mind approaching twenty.
Full of intellect, intrigue, adventure
Which passing years could never censure.

PART SIX

POEMS NOT INCLUDED IN PARTS 1,2,3,4 AND 5

AN END TO ANOREXIA

She's building a mountain of chips,
Still shovelling from the tray.
On the subject - the girth of one's hips,
She does not have a lot to say.

She's adding a tubeful of sauce
And eyeing the chicken parilla.
For a moment she'll stick to this course
With a sizeable side of tortilla.

He's having a splash at the soup,
Contemplating the loaf in one bite.
His appetite set for the coup
-The destruction of all food in sight.

An insult to taste this small plate,
Set to temper his gnawing advance.
But in filling it six times to date,
He is keen to take more than one chance.

Together they finish their feast,
Their delight made complete in the filling.
The grinding of jaws has ceased
-There's more but the stomach's not willing.

Our gourmet friends are large not fat,
Good food is for our pleasure.
It's important to remember that
We were not made to measure.

THE GUT

The last bastion of the male preserve,
A fruit of indulgence
Developed over years,
Fed upon a nutrient rich assortment
Of beer, chips and indolence, is the gut.
Nurtured from a tiny swelling seedling,
Fast breeders may force feed,
Most opt for a steady increase of excess.
An outcome comes out,
First showing as a curled lip
Spilling over trouser belt,
Then ballooning in time
To accommodate the waste in life,
Finally forming a baby stomach
Attached to the proud father
And so attractive to the female of the species.

THE SPILLAGE

I saw it all,
The place was deserted.
I greet him.
He hovers to a table,
One for two.
Orders coffee and toast.

Busying myself I observe
From time to time
The feeding habit.
Insignificant, secondary
To his reading matter.
Barely conscious,
Floating in a sea of words.

Coaxing coffee
Between the lips
Hardly visible
Beneath the beard,
Harbouring crumbs,
Nesting as tiny eggs.

He misses and dribbles,
A little stream runs
Amid gaps in hair,
Surfacing upon the chin.

He is aware
Of some irritation
Not looking,
Mechanically wipes away,
Catching coffee cup.
Upsetting to see
Coffee collecting
On table top.
Choking at the sight,
His mouthful explodes
And a nasal spray
Patterns the wall.
Panics with the cup,
Sets coffee pot on edge,
Covers clothing
A burning brown.
Arises to flee
The wreckage.

A few seconds,
Beginning to end.
I help him
To clean up.
He makes me promise
Not to tell.
I swear I won't
And I didn't,
Plenty of men wear beards.

DUMPED

You pick out the swelling,
Watch it developing,
It's all in the timing.

And then you're turning,
Arms ferocious flailing,
Feet flipper beating.

Wave upon your arching,
Six feet above menacing,
For a second water balancing.

Crashing down upon you,
Turns the body right around,
Almost breaks the back.
Lost in a foam bath,
Bumping along the bottom,
Washed up in the surf,
You find your breath again.

SHOPPING FOR SHOES

There was an old woman who lived in a shoe,
I can believe it.
Today the world is a shoe,
At least it seems that way,
Treading the paths of fashion footwear.
Numb as my reflection, static
In a series of shop fronts.
Drifting in a haze of leather and suede,
Of brown and black.
High and low heels,
Laced up or slipped on,
They pinch a little, rub her up the wrong way.

I drop out, a broken man,
Jellied under the crushing heel
Of a thousand different designs.

From the pavement fascinated
By the foot fall
Of a thousand passers by,
Each one of them occupying
A different pair.

THE RACE

Fingers drumming on plastic fascia.
Eyes straining for crumpled newspaper.
Feet twitch, pushing the pedals,
An idling body ready for action.

Undercurrent of electricity,
Four minutes before they open the store.
Suspense, the ensuing battle, killing me
But calm - you have a trusted strategy.

The attendant appears, revolving doors.
A push from the front line,
The rearguard section follows.
Still I wait, poised to pounce.

Slowly, slowly I advance - then crash!
The trolley speeds ahead,
Weaving as a homing missile
Driven by some unearthly force.

Others cause collisions, form queues, not me.
No time for the tail back
Forming in fresh fruit and vegetables,
Employing my park and pick policy.

Kids perch on slow-moving loads,
Amateurs out for a family run.
Wasting time weighing up produce,
Overtaken by the desire for perfection.

Professionally plucking cans from preset locations,
I make for the head of the field.
Through bakery, fresh meat, frozen and fish,
Arriving front runner at dairy department.

Through beverages, one last push to the line.
One till working, I am there
Sharing my success with the young cashier,
Suitably impressed by another polished performance.

TIGHTROPE

Tip-toe along this eyeliner path
Drawn between a chilling channel of water
And a terrible death,
A thousand metre fall to the nearest cafe,
A tumble through flimsy shrub
And stunning rock
And flying dust,
All to the tune of a terrifying scream.
The channels which run in my head,
What if they turn me dizzy?
The low-flying clouds,
What if there's a white out?
Then my feet will fail, fall
And the rest of my body with me,
But for now I am dancing the Madeiran way
-Doing the levada.

CHEWING GUM, BRACE AND TEETH

American girls atop fairy toadstools,
Chewing gum, brace and teeth,
Go Mexican, burrito and quesadilla,
Still smiling through each mouthful.
Gawky, awkward, their physical form
Denying the youth which passed them by
And remains to be seen
Keenly observed in the light of their faces.
Missing manners, protégés of their country's art,
Leaving left overs but buying more
Candy, shake and ice cream,
Starting their slow middle-aged spread.